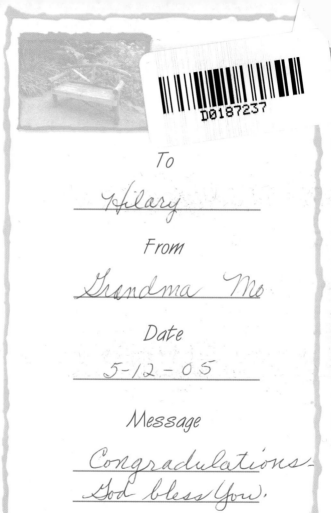

To

Hilary

From

Grandma Mo

Date

_5-12-05_

Message

Congradulations-
God bless You.

Proverbs to Live By

© 2003 Christian Art Gifts, RSA
          Christian Art Gifts Inc., IL, USA

Compiled by Wilma Le Roux
Designed by Christian Art Gifts

ISBN 1-86920-064-0

Printed in China

05 06 07 08 09 10 11 12 – 11 10 9 8 7 6

Proverbs
to live by

christian
art gifts

Contents

He that is soon angry dealeth foolishly: and a man of wicked devices is hated.

Proverbs 14:17 (KJV)

He who is slow to wrath has great understanding, but he who is impulsive exalts folly.

Proverbs 14:29 (NKJV)

A soft answer turns away wrath, but a harsh word stirs up anger.

Proverbs 15:1 (ESV)

A wrathful man stirreth up strife: but he that is slow to anger appeaseth strife.

Proverbs 15:18 (KJV)

Whoever is slow to anger is better than the mighty, and he who rules his spirit than he who takes a city.

Proverbs 16:32 (ESV)

Anger

A man of great wrath will suffer punishment; for if you rescue him, you will have to do it again.

Proverbs 19:19 (NKJV)

A gift in secret pacifieth anger: and a reward in the bosom strong wrath.

Proverbs 21:14 (KJV)

Whoever sows injustice will reap calamity, and the rod of his fury will fail.

Proverbs 22:8 (ESV)

Do not make friends with a hot-tempered man, do not associate with one easily angered, or you may learn his ways and get yourself ensnared.

Proverbs 22:24-25 (NIV)

An angry man stirs up strife, and a furious man abounds in transgression.

Proverbs 29:22 (NKJV)

My son, if sinners entice you, do not give in to them.

Proverbs 1:10 (NIV)

Do not enter the path of the wicked, and do not walk in the way of the evil. Avoid it; do not go on it; turn away from it and pass on. For they cannot sleep unless they have done wrong; they are robbed of sleep unless they have made someone stumble. For they eat the bread of wickedness and drink the wine of violence.

Proverbs 4:14-17 (ESV)

He that tilleth his land shall be satisfied with bread: but he that followeth vain persons is void of understanding.

Proverbs 12:11 (KJV)

He who walks with wise men will be wise, but the companion of fools will be destroyed.

Proverbs 13:20 (NKJV)

Associates

A violent man entices his neighbor, and leads him in a way that is not good. He winks his eye to devise perverse things; he purses his lips and brings about evil.

Proverbs 16:29-30 (NKJV)

Be not envious of evil men, nor desire to be with them, for their hearts devise violence, and their lips talk of trouble.

Proverbs 24:1-2 (ESV)

He who keeps the law is a discerning son, but a companion of gluttons disgraces his father.

Proverbs 28:7 (NIV)

Whoso loveth wisdom rejoiceth his father: but he that keepeth company with harlots spendeth his substance.

Proverbs 29:3 (KJV)

Happy is the man who finds wisdom, and the man who gains understanding.

Proverbs 3:13 (NIV)

The LORD blesseth the habitation of the just.

Proverbs 3:33 (KJV)

Now then, my sons, listen to me; blessed are those who keep my ways. Blessed is the man who listens to me, watching daily at my doors, waiting at my doorway.

Proverbs 8:32, 34 (NIV)

Blessings are on the head of the righteous, but violence covers the mouth of the wicked. The memory of the righteous is blessed, but the name of the wicked will rot.

Proverbs 10:6-7 (NKJV)

The blessing of the LORD makes rich, and he adds no sorrow with it.

Proverbs 10:22 (ESV)

Blessing

By the blessing of the upright a city is exalted, but by the mouth of the wicked it is overthrown.

Proverbs 11:11 (ESV)

The people will curse him who withholds grain, but blessing will be on the head of him who sells it.

Proverbs 11:26 (NKJV)

Whoever gives heed to instruction prospers, and blessed is he who trusts in the LORD.

Proverbs 16:20 (NIV)

But it will go well with those who convict the guilty, and rich blessing will come upon them.

Proverbs 24:25 (NIV)

Blessed is the one who fears the LORD always, but whoever hardens his heart will fall into calamity.

Proverbs 28:14 (ESV)

The labor of the righteous leads to life, the wages of the wicked to sin.

Proverbs 10:16 (NKJV)

The LORD abhors dishonest scales, but accurate weights are his delight.

Proverbs 11:1 (NIV)

Wealth gotten by vanity shall be diminished: but he that gathereth by labour shall increase.

Proverbs 13:11 (KJV)

The person who labors, labors for himself, for his hungry mouth drives him on.

Proverbs 16:26 (NKJV)

"Bad, Bad," says the buyer, but when he goes away, then he boasts.

Proverbs 20:14 (ESV)

Business

Bread gained by deceit is sweet to a man, but afterward his mouth will be full of gravel.

Proverbs 20:17 (ESV)

Seest thou a man diligent in his business? He shall stand before kings; he shall not stand before mean men.

Proverbs 22:29 (KJV)

Buy the truth and do not sell it; get wisdom, discipline and understanding.

Proverbs 23:23 (NIV)

Prepare your work outside; get everything ready for yourself in the field, and after that build your house.

Proverbs 24:27 (ESV)

She considers a field and buys it; from her profits she plants a vineyard.

Proverbs 31:16 (NKJV)

For the lips of an adulteress drip honey, and her speech is smoother than oil; but in the end she is bitter as gall, sharp as a double-edged sword. Her feet go down to death; her steps lead straight to the grave.

Proverbs 5:3-5 (NIV)

For whoever finds me finds life, and obtains favor from the LORD; but he who sins against me wrongs his own soul; all those who hate me love death.

Proverbs 8:35-36 (NKJV)

Riches profit not in the day of wrath: but righteousness delivereth from death.

Proverbs 11:4 (KJV)

When a wicked man dies, his expectation will perish, and the hope of the unjust perishes.

Proverbs 11:7 (NKJV)

Death

Whoever is steadfast in righteousness will live, but he who pursues evil will die.

Proverbs 11:19 (ESV)

In the way of righteousness there is life; along that path is immortality.

Proverbs 12:28 (NIV)

Correction is grievous unto him that forsaketh the way: and he that hateth reproof shall die.

Proverbs 15:10 (KJV)

He who keeps the commandment keeps his soul, but he who is careless of his ways will die.

Proverbs 19:16 (NKJV)

A man who strays from the path of understanding comes to rest in the company of the dead.

Proverbs 21:16 (NIV)

A scoundrel and villain, who goes about with a corrupt mouth, who plots evil with deceit in his heart – he always stirs up dissension.

Proverbs 6:12, 14 (NIV)

The thoughts of the righteous are just; the counsels of the wicked are deceitful.

Proverbs 12:5 (ESV)

Deceit is in the heart of those who devise evil, but those who plan peace have joy.

Proverbs 12:20 (ESV)

A true witness delivereth souls: but a deceitful witness speaketh lies.

Proverbs 14:25 (KJV)

He who has a deceitful heart finds no good, and he who has a perverse tongue falls into evil.

Proverbs 17:20 (NKJV)

Deceit

Do not testify against your neighbor without cause, or use your lips to deceive. Do not say, "I'll do to him as he has done to me; I'll pay that man back for what he did."

Proverbs 24:28-29 (NIV)

Like the glaze covering an earthen vessel are fervent lips with an evil heart. Whoever hates disguises himself with his lips and harbors deceit in his heart; when he speaks graciously, believe him not, for there are seven abominations in his heart; though his hatred be covered with deception, his wickedness will be exposed in the assembly.

Proverbs 26:23-26 (ESV)

Faithful are the wounds of a friend, but the kisses of an enemy are deceitful.

Proverbs 27:6 (NKJV)

Discretion shall preserve thee, understanding shall keep thee: to deliver thee from the way of the evil man, from the man that speaketh froward things.

Proverbs 2:11-12 (KJV)

Treasures gained by wickedness do not profit, but righteousness delivers from death.

Proverbs 10:2 (ESV)

The righteousness of the upright delivers them, but the unfaithful are trapped by evil desires.

Proverbs 11:6 (NIV)

The righteous is delivered from trouble, and it comes to the wicked instead.

Proverbs 11:8 (NKJV)

The words of the wicked are, "Lie in wait for blood," but the mouth of the upright will deliver them.

Proverbs 12:6 (NKJV)

Deliverance

A true witness delivereth souls: but a deceitful witness speaketh lies.

Proverbs 14:25 (KJV)

Do not say, "I will repay evil"; wait for the LORD, and he will deliver you.

Proverbs 20:22 (ESV)

The horse is prepared for the day of battle, but deliverance is of the LORD.

Proverbs 21:31 (NKJV)

Thou shalt beat him with the rod, and shalt deliver his soul from hell.

Proverbs 23:14 (KJV)

Whoever walks blamelessly will be saved, but he who is perverse will suddenly fall.

Proverbs 28:18 (NKJV)

He who trusts in himself is a fool, but he who walks in wisdom is kept safe.

Proverbs 28:26 (NIV)

Desire

Happy is the man that findeth wisdom. She is more precious than rubies: all the things thou canst desire are not to be compared unto her.

Proverbs 3:13, 15 (KJV)

Choose knowledge rather than choice gold, for wisdom is more precious than rubies, and nothing you desire can compare with her.

Proverbs 8:10-11 (NIV)

What the wicked dreads will come upon him, but the desire of the righteous will be granted.

Proverbs 10:24 (ESV)

The desire of the righteous is only good: but the expectation of the wicked is wrath.

Proverbs 11:23 (KJV)

Hope deferred makes the heart sick, but when the desire comes, it is a tree of life.

Proverbs 13:12 (NKJV)

Desire

A longing fulfilled is sweet to the soul, but fools detest turning from evil.

Proverbs 13:19 (NIV)

Through desire a man, having separated himself, seeketh and intermeddleth with all wisdom.

Proverbs 18:1 (KJV)

The desire of the lazy man kills him, for his hands refuse to labor. He covets greedily all day long, but the righteous gives and does not spare.

Proverbs 21:25-26 (NKJV)

Eat thou not the bread of him that hath an evil eye, neither desire thou his dainty meats.

Proverbs 23:6 (KJV)

Be not thou envious against evil men, neither desire to be with them.

Proverbs 24:1 (KJV)

Diligence

Keep thy heart with all diligence; for out of it are the issues of life.

Proverbs 4:23 (KJV)

He who gathers in summer is a wise son; he who sleeps in harvest is a son who causes shame.

Proverbs 10:5 (NKJV)

The hand of the diligent will rule, while the slothful will be put to forced labor.

Proverbs 12:24 (ESV)

The lazy man does not roast his game, but the diligent man prizes his possessions.

Proverbs 12:27 (NIV)

The plans of the diligent lead surely to abundance, but everyone who is hasty comes only to poverty.

Proverbs 21:5 (ESV)

Diligence

Do you see a man who excels in his work? He will stand before kings; he will not stand before unknown men.

Proverbs 22:29 (NKJV)

If you say, "Behold, we did not know this," does not he who weighs the heart perceive it? Does not he who keeps watch over your soul know it, and will he not repay man according to his work?

Proverbs 24:12 (ESV)

Be diligent to know the state of your flocks, and attend to your herds.

Proverbs 27:23 (NKJV)

She seeks wool and flax, and willingly works with her hands. She also rises while it is yet night, and provides food for her household. She watches over the ways of her household, and does not eat the bread of idleness.

Proverbs 31:13, 15, 27 (NKJV)

My son, do not go along with them, do not set foot on their paths; for their feet rush into sin, they are swift to shed blood.

Proverbs 1:15-16 (NIV)

Wisdom will save you from the ways of wicked men, from men whose words are perverse, who leave the straight paths to walk in dark ways, who delight in doing wrong and rejoice in the perverseness of evil, whose paths are crooked and who are devious in their ways.

Proverbs 2:12-15 (NIV)

Be not wise in thine own eyes: fear the LORD, and depart from evil.

Proverbs 3:7 (KJV)

Devise not evil against thy neighbour, seeing he dwelleth securely by thee.

Proverbs 3:29 (KJV)

Evil

Do not enter the path of the wicked, and do not walk in the way of the evil.

Proverbs 4:14 (ESV)

The evil deeds of a wicked man ensnare him; the cords of his sin hold him fast.

Proverbs 5: 22 (NIV)

A scoundrel and villain, who goes about with a corrupt mouth, who plots evil with deceit in his heart – he always stirs up dissension. Therefore disaster will overtake him in an instant; he will suddenly be destroyed – without remedy.

Proverbs 6:12, 14-15 (NIV)

The fear of the LORD is to hate evil: pride, and arrogancy, and the evil way, and the froward mouth, do I hate.

Proverbs 8:13 (KJV)

Whoever is steadfast in righteousness will live, but he who pursues evil will die. Be assured, an evil person will not go unpunished, but the offspring of the righteous will be delivered.

Proverbs 11:19, 21 (ESV)

He who seeks good finds goodwill, but evil comes to him who searches for it.

Proverbs 11:27 (NIV)

A good man obtaineth favour of the LORD: but a man of wicked devices will he condemn.

Proverbs 12:2 (KJV)

The evil bow before the good; and the wicked at the gates of the righteous.

Proverbs 14:19 (KJV)

Do they not err that devise evil? But mercy and truth shall be to them that devise good.

Proverbs 14:22 (KJV)

Evil

The heart of the righteous studieth to answer: but the mouth of the wicked poureth out evil things.

Proverbs 15:28 (KJV)

An ungodly man digs up evil, and it is on his lips like a burning fire.

Proverbs 16:27 (NKJV)

The soul of the wicked desires evil; his neighbor finds no mercy in his eyes.

Proverbs 21:10 (ESV)

Be not thou envious against evil men, neither desire to be with them.

Proverbs 24:1 (KJV)

Evil men do not understand justice, but those who seek the LORD understand all.

Proverbs 28:5 (NKJV)

He keepeth the paths of judgment, and preserveth the way of his saints.

Proverbs 2:8 (KJV)

Let not steadfast love and faithfulness forsake you; bind them around your neck; write them on the tablet of your heart.

Proverbs 3:3 (ESV)

A talebearer reveals secrets, but he who is of a faithful spirit conceals a matter.

Proverbs 11:13 (NKJV)

A wicked messenger falls into trouble, but a faithful envoy brings healing.

Proverbs 13:17 (ESV)

A faithful witness will not lie: but a false witness will utter lies.

Proverbs 14:5 (KJV)

Faithfulness

By steadfast love and faithfulness iniquity is atoned for, and by the fear of the LORD one turns away from evil.

Proverbs 16:6 (ESV)

Steadfast love and faithfulness preserve the king, and by steadfast love his throne is upheld.

Proverbs 20:28 (ESV)

Like the cold of snow in time of harvest is a faithful messenger to those who send him, for he refreshes the soul of his masters.

Proverbs 25:13 (NKJV)

Faithful are the wounds of a friend; profuse are the kisses of an enemy.

Proverbs 27:6 (ESV)

A faithful man shall abound with blessings: but he that maketh haste to be rich shall not be innocent.

Proverbs 28:20 (KJV)

Hear, my son, your father's instruction, and forsake not your mother's teaching, for they are a graceful garland for your head and pendants for your neck.

Proverbs 1:8-9 (ESV)

My son, do not despise the LORD's discipline and do not resent his rebuke, because the LORD disciplines those he loves, as a father the son he delights in.

Proverbs 3:11-12 (NIV)

Hear, ye children, the instruction of a father, and attend to know understanding. For I give you good doctrine, forsake ye not my law. For I was my father's son, tender and only beloved in the sight of my mother. He taught me also, and said unto me, let thine heart retain my words: keep my commandments, and live.

Proverbs 4:1-4 (KJV)

Family

My son, keep your father's commands and do not forsake your mother's teaching.

Proverbs 6:20 (NIV)

He who spares his rod hates his son, but he who loves him disciplines him promptly.

Proverbs 13:24 (NKJV)

Grandchildren are the crown of the aged, and the glory of children is their fathers.

Proverbs 17:6 (ESV)

Houses and riches are an inheritance from fathers, but a prudent wife is from the LORD.

Proverbs 19:14 (NKJV)

He who robs his father and drives out his mother is a son who brings shame and disgrace.

Proverbs 19:26 (NIV)

Whoso curseth his father or his mother, his lamp shall be put out in obscure darkness.

Proverbs 20:20 (KJV)

Train a child in the way he should go, and when he is old he will not turn from it.

Proverbs 22:6 (NIV)

Listen to your father who gave you life, and do not despise your mother when she is old.

Proverbs 23:22 (ESV)

The rod and reproof give wisdom: but a child left to himself bringeth his mother to shame.

Proverbs 29:15 (KJV)

The eye that mocks his father, and scorns obedience to his mother, the ravens of the valley will pick it out, and the young eagles will eat it.

Proverbs 30:17 (NKJV)

Fear of the Lord

The fear of the LORD is the beginning of knowledge: but fools despise wisdom and instruction.

Proverbs 1:7 (KJV)

Then they will call upon me, but I will not answer; they will seek me diligently but will not find me. Because they hated knowledge and did not choose the fear of the LORD.

Proverbs 1:28-29 (ESV)

My son, if you receive my words, and treasure my commands within you, then you will understand the fear of the LORD, and find the knowledge of God.

Proverbs 2:1, 5 (NKJV)

Be not wise in your own eyes; fear the LORD, and turn away from evil.

Proverbs 3:7 (ESV)

The fear of the LORD prolongeth days: but the years of the wicked shall be shortened.

Proverbs 10:27 (KJV)

He who fears the LORD has a secure fortress, and for his children it will be a refuge. The fear of the LORD is a fountain of life, turning a man from the snares of death.

Proverbs 14:26-27 (NIV)

Better is a little with the fear of the LORD than great treasure and trouble with it.

Proverbs 15:16 (ESV)

By humility and the fear of the LORD are riches and honor and life.

Proverbs 22:4 (NKJV)

Let not thine heart envy sinners: but be thou in the fear of the LORD all the day long.

Proverbs 23:17 (KJV)

The wise in heart will receive commandments: but a prating fool shall fall.

Proverbs 10:8 (KJV)

The lips of the righteous feed many, but fools die for lack of sense.

Proverbs 10:21 (ESV)

The way of a fool seems right to him, but a wise man listens to advice.

Proverbs 12:15 (NIV)

Every prudent man dealeth with knowledge: but a fool layeth open his folly.

Proverbs 13:16 (KJV)

A fool despises his father's instruction, but whoever heeds reproof is prudent.

Proverbs 15:5 (ESV)

Rebuke is more effective for a wise man than a hundred blows on a fool.

Proverbs 17:10 (NKJV)

Better to meet a bear robbed of her cubs than a fool in his folly.

Proverbs 17:12 (NIV)

Why should a fool have money in his hand to buy wisdom when he has no sense?

Proverbs 17:16 (ESV)

Even a fool is thought wise if he keeps silent, and discerning if he holds his tongue.

Proverbs 17:28 (NIV)

A fool has no delight in understanding, but in expressing his own heart.

Proverbs 18:2 (NKJV)

Better is the poor that walketh in his integrity, than he that is perverse in his lips, and is a fool.

Proverbs 19:1 (KJV)

Do not speak in the hearing of a fool, for he will despise the good sense of your words.

Proverbs 23:9 (ESV)

Wisdom is too high for a fool: he openeth not his mouth in the gate.

Proverbs 24:7 (KJV)

As snow in summer and rain in harvest, so honor is not fitting for a fool.

Proverbs 26:1 (NKJV)

Like an archer who wounds everybody is one who hires a passing fool or drunkard.

Proverbs 26:10 (ESV)

As a dog returns to his own vomit, so a fool repeats his folly.

Proverbs 26:11 (NKJV)

Though you grind a fool in a mortar, you will not remove his folly from him.

Proverbs 27:22 (NIV)

My son, if you have put up security for your neighbor, have given your pledge for a stranger, then do this, my son, and save yourself, for you have come into the hand of your neighbor: go, hasten, and plead urgently with your neighbor.

Proverbs 6:1, 3 (ESV)

When a man's ways please the LORD, he maketh even his enemies to be at peace with him.

Proverbs 16:7 (KJV)

A friend loves at all times, and a brother is born for adversity.

Proverbs 17:17 (NIV)

A man who has friends must himself be friendly, but there is a friend who sticks closer than a brother.

Proverbs 18:24 (NKJV)

Friends and enemies

Many will intreat the favour of the prince: and every man is a friend to him that giveth gifts.

Proverbs 19:6 (KJV)

Make no friendship with an angry man, and with a furious man do not go, lest you learn his ways and set a snare for your soul.

Proverbs 22:24-25 (NKJV)

Do not gloat when your enemy falls; when he stumbles, do not let your heart rejoice, or the LORD will see and disapprove and turn his wrath away from him.

Proverbs 24:17-18 (NIV)

If thine enemy be hungry, give him bread to eat; and if he be thirsty, give him water to drink: For thou shalt heap coals of fire upon his head, and the LORD shall reward thee.

Proverbs 25:21-22 (KJV)

Faithful are the wounds of a friend; profuse are the kisses of an enemy.

Proverbs 27:6 (ESV)

Ointment and perfume delight the heart, and the sweetness of a man's friend gives delight by hearty counsel.

Proverbs 27:9 (NKJV)

Do not forsake your friend and the friend of your father, and do not go to your brother's house when disaster strikes you – better a neighbor nearby than a brother far away.

Proverbs 27:10 (NIV)

As iron sharpens iron, so a man sharpens the countenance of his friend.

Proverbs 27:17 (NKJV)

Generosity

Do not say to your neighbor, "Go, and come again, tomorrow I will give it" – when you have it with you.

Proverbs 3:28 (ESV)

There is one who scatters, yet increases more; and there is one who withholds more than is right, but it leads to poverty. The generous soul will be made rich, and he who waters will also be watered himself.

Proverbs 11:24-25 (NKJV)

Whoever despises his neighbor is a sinner, but blessed is he who is generous to the poor. Whoever oppresses a poor man insults his Maker, but he who is generous to the needy honors him.

Proverbs 14:21, 31 (ESV)

Generosity

He who has pity on the poor lends to the LORD, and He will pay back what he has given.

Proverbs 19:17 (NKJV)

A generous man will himself be blessed, for he shares his food with the poor.

Proverbs 22:9 (NIV)

Like clouds and wind without rain is a man who boasts of gifts he does not give.

Proverbs 25:14 (NIV)

If your enemy is hungry, give him bread to eat; and if he is thirsty, give him water to drink; for so you will heap coals of fire on his head, and the LORD will reward you.

Proverbs 25:21-22 (NKJV)

Whoever gives to the poor will not want, but he who hides his eyes will get many a curse.

Proverbs 28:27 (ESV)

Goodness

Thus you will walk in the ways of good men and keep to the paths of the righteous. For the upright will live in the land, and the blameless will remain in it; but the wicked will be cut off from the land, and the unfaithful will be torn from it.

Proverbs 2:20-22 (NIV)

Withhold not good from them to whom it is due, when it is in the power of thine hand to do it.

Proverbs 3:27 (KJV)

The desire of the righteous is only good, but the expectation of the wicked is wrath.

Proverbs 11:23 (NKJV)

He that diligently seeketh good procureth favour: but he that seeketh mischief, it shall come unto him.

Proverbs 11:27 (KJV)

A good man obtaineth favour of the Lᴏʀᴅ: but a man of wicked devices will he condemn.

Proverbs 12:2 (KJV)

From the fruit of his lips a man is filled with good things as surely as the work of his hands rewards him.

Proverbs 12:14 (NIV)

Heaviness in the heart of man maketh it stoop: but a good word maketh it glad.

Proverbs 12:25 (KJV)

Good sense wins favor, but the way of the treacherous is their ruin.

Proverbs 13:15 (ESV)

The backslider in heart will be filled with his own ways, but a good man will be satisfied from above.

Proverbs 14:14 (NKJV)

Goodness

The evil bow before the good; and the wicked at the gates of the righteous.

Proverbs 14:19 (KJV)

Do not those who plot evil go astray? But those who plan what is good find love and faithfulness.

Proverbs 14:22 (NIV)

He who heeds the word wisely will find good, and whoever trusts in the LORD, happy is he.

Proverbs 16:20 (NKJV)

If anyone returns evil for good, evil will not depart from his house.

Proverbs 17:13 (ESV)

He who gets wisdom loves his own soul; he who keeps understanding will find good.

Proverbs 19:8 (NKJV)

My son, eat thou honey, because it is good; and the honeycomb, which is sweet to thy taste: So shall the knowledge of wisdom be unto thy soul: when thou hast found it, then there shall be a reward, and thy expectation shall not be cut off.

Proverbs 24:13-14 (KJV)

Whoever misleads the upright into an evil way will fall into his own pit, but the blameless will have a goodly inheritance.

Proverbs 28:10 (ESV)

A wife of noble character who can find? She is worth far more than rubies. Her husband has full confidence in her and lacks nothing of value. She brings him good, not harm, all the days of her life.

Proverbs 31:10-12 (NIV)

Gossip

A talebearer reveals secrets, but he who is of a faithful spirit conceals a matter.

Proverbs 11:13 (NKJV)

Whoever speaks the truth gives honest evidence, but a false witness utters deceit.

Proverbs 12:17 (ESV)

A perverse man stirs up dissension, and a gossip separates close friends.

Proverbs 16:28 (NIV)

The words of a talebearer are like tasty trifles, and they go down into the inmost body.

Proverbs 18:8 (NKJV)

He that goeth about as a talebearer revealeth secrets: therefore meddle not with him that flattereth with his lips.

Proverbs 20:19 (KJV)

For lack of wood the fire goes out, and where there is no whisperer, quarreling ceases.

Proverbs 26:20 (ESV)

The words of a gossip are like choice morsels; they go down to a man's inmost parts. Like a coating of glaze over earthenware are fervent lips with an evil heart.

Proverbs 26:22-23 (NIV)

He that hateth dissembleth with his lips, and layeth up deceit within him; when he speaketh fair, believe him not: for there are seven abominations in his heart.

Proverbs 26:24-25 (KJV)

Do not slander a servant to his master, or he will curse you, and you will pay for it.

Proverbs 30:10 (NIV)

Government

By me kings reign, and rulers decree what is just; by me princes rule, and nobles, all who govern justly.

Proverbs 8:15-16 (ESV)

The lips of a king speak as an oracle, and his mouth should not betray justice.

Proverbs 16:10 (NIV)

Righteous lips are the delight of kings; and they love him that speaketh right.

Proverbs 16:13 (KJV)

A king's rage is like the roar of a lion, but his favor is like dew on the grass.

Proverbs 19:12 (NIV)

A king who sits on the throne of judgment scatters all evil with his eyes.

Proverbs 20:8 (NKJV)

A wise king winnows out the wicked; he drives the threshing wheel over them.

Proverbs 20:26 (NIV)

Mercy and truth preserve the king: and his throne is upholden by mercy.

Proverbs 20:28 (KJV)

The king's heart is in the hand of the LORD; he directs it like a watercourse wherever he pleases.

Proverbs 21:1 (NIV)

It is the glory of God to conceal a thing: but the honour of kings is to search out a matter.

Proverbs 25:2 (KJV)

The king establishes the land by justice.

Proverbs 29:4 (NKJV)

The king that faithfully judgeth the poor, his throne shall be established for ever.

Proverbs 29:14 (KJV)

Guidance

Let the wise hear and increase in learning, and the one who understands obtain guidance, to understand a proverb and a saying, the words of the wise and their riddles.

Proverbs 1:5-6 (ESV)

I guide you in the way of wisdom and lead you along straight paths.

Proverbs 4:11 (NIV)

My son, keep your father's command, and do not forsake the law of your mother. When you roam, they will lead you; when you sleep, they will keep you; and when you awake, they will speak with you. For the commandment is a lamp, and the law a light; reproofs of instruction are the way of life.

Proverbs 6:20, 22-23 (NKJV)

The integrity of the upright shall guide them: but the perverseness of transgressors shall destroy them.

Proverbs 11:3 (KJV)

Where there is no counsel, the people fall; but in the multitude of counselors there is safety.

Proverbs 11:14 (NKJV)

A wise man's heart guides his mouth, and his lips promote instruction.

Proverbs 16:23 (NIV)

Plans are established by counsel; by wise guidance wage war.

Proverbs 20:18 (ESV)

A man's steps are directed by the LORD. How then can anyone understand his own way?

Proverbs 20:24 (NIV)

Hatred

The fear of the LORD is hatred of evil. Pride and arrogance and the way of evil and perverted speech I hate.

Proverbs 8:13 (ESV)

But he that sinneth against me wrongeth his own soul: all they that hate me love death.

Proverbs 8:36 (KJV)

Hatred stirs up dissension, but love covers over all wrongs.

Proverbs 10:12 (NIV)

Whoever loves instruction loves knowledge, but he who hates correction is stupid.

Proverbs 12:1 (NKJV)

Whoever spares the rod hates his son.

Proverbs 13:24 (ESV)

Better is a dinner of herbs where love is, than a fatted calf with hatred.

Proverbs 15:17 (NKJV)

Hatred

A greedy man brings trouble to his family, but he who hates bribes will live.

Proverbs 15:27 (NIV)

Let your foot be seldom in your neighbor's house, lest he have his fill of you and hate you.

Proverbs 25:17 (ESV)

He who hates, disguises it with his lips, and lays up deceit within himself; though his hatred is covered by deceit, his wickedness will be revealed before the assembly.

Proverbs 26:24, 26 (NKJV)

The bloodthirsty hate the upright: but the just seek his soul.

Proverbs 29:10 (KJV)

The partner of a thief hates his own life; he hears the curse, but discloses nothing.

Proverbs 29:24 (ESV)

Honor and glory

Honor the LORD with your wealth, with the firstfruits of all your crops; then your barns will be filled to overflowing, and your vats will brim over with new wine.

Proverbs 3:9-10 (NIV)

The wise shall inherit glory, but shame shall be the legacy of fools.

Proverbs 3:35 (NKJV)

A gracious woman retaineth honour: and strong men retain riches.

Proverbs 11:16 (KJV)

Poverty and shame will come to him who disdains correction, but he who regards a rebuke will be honored.

Proverbs 13:18 (NKJV)

It is an honor for a man to keep aloof from strife, but every fool will be quarreling.

Proverbs 20:3 (ESV)

The glory of young men is their strength, gray hair the splendor of the old.

Proverbs 20:29 (NIV)

It is the glory of God to conceal things, but the glory of kings is to search things out.

Proverbs 25:2 (ESV)

It is not good to eat too much honey, nor is it honorable to seek one's own honor.

Proverbs 25:27 (NIV)

As snow in summer, and as rain in harvest, so honour is not seemly for a fool.

Proverbs 26:1 (KJV)

Whoever tends a fig tree will eat its fruit, and he who guards his master will be honored.

Proverbs 27:18 (ESV)

When righteous men do rejoice, there is great glory.

Proverbs 28:12 (KJV)

Hope

The hope of the righteous brings joy, but the expectation of the wicked will perish.

Proverbs 10:28 (ESV)

When a wicked man dies, his expectation will perish, and the hope of the unjust perishes.

Proverbs 11:7 (NKJV)

The desire of the righteous ends only in good, but the hope of the wicked only in wrath.

Proverbs 11:23 (NIV)

Hope deferred maketh the heart sick: but when the desire cometh, it is a tree of life.

Proverbs 13:12 (KJV)

The wicked is driven away in his wickedness: but the righteous hath hope in his death.

Proverbs 14:32 (KJV)

Chasten your son while there is hope, and do not set your heart on his destruction.

Proverbs 19:18 (NKJV)

Surely there is a future, and your hope will not be cut off.

Proverbs 23:18 (ESV)

So shall the knowledge of wisdom be unto thy soul: when thou hast found it, then there shall be a reward, and thy expectation shall not be cut off.

Proverbs 24:14 (KJV)

For there will be no prospect for the evil man; the lamp of the wicked will be put out.

Proverbs 24:20 (NKJV)

Do you see a man who is wise in his own eyes? There is more hope for a fool than for him.

Proverbs 26:12 (ESV)

Do you see a man who speaks in haste? There is more hope for a fool than for him.

Proverbs 29:20 (NIV)

Surely He scorns the scornful, but gives grace to the humble.

Proverbs 3:34 (NKJV)

There are six things that the LORD hates, seven that are an abomination to him: haughty eyes, a lying tongue, and hands that shed innocent blood, a heart that devises wicked plans, feet that make haste to run to evil, a false witness who breathes out lies, and one who sows discord among brothers.

Proverbs 6:16-19 (ESV)

The fear of the LORD is to hate evil: pride, and arrogancy, and the evil way, and the froward mouth, do I hate.

Proverbs 8:13 (KJV)

When pride comes, then comes disgrace, but with humility comes wisdom.

Proverbs 11:2 (NIV)

Pride only breeds quarrels, but wisdom is found in those who take advice.

Proverbs 13:10 (NIV)

The LORD will destroy the house of the proud, but He will establish the boundary of the widow.

Proverbs 15:25 (NKJV)

The fear of the LORD is instruction in wisdom, and humility comes before honor.

Proverbs 15:33 (ESV)

Every one that is proud in heart is an abomination to the LORD: though hand join in hand, he shall not be unpunished.

Proverbs 16:5 (KJV)

Pride goeth before destruction, and an haughty spirit before a fall. Better it is to be of an humble spirit with the lowly, than to divide the spoil with the proud.

Proverbs 16:18-19 (KJV)

Humility and pride

Before his downfall a man's heart is proud, but humility comes before honor.

Proverbs 18:12 (NIV)

A haughty look, a proud heart, and the plowing of the wicked are sin.

Proverbs 21:4 (NKJV)

"Scoffer" is the name of the arrogant, haughty man who acts with arrogant pride.

Proverbs 21:24 (ESV)

By humility and the fear of the LORD are riches, and honour, and life.

Proverbs 22:4 (KJV)

Do not boast about tomorrow, for you do not know what a day may bring forth.

Proverbs 27:1 (NIV)

Let another praise you, and not your own mouth; a stranger, and not your own lips.

Proverbs 27:2 (ESV)

As the fining pot for silver, and the furnace for gold; so is a man to his praise.

Proverbs 27:21 (KJV)

A man's pride will bring him low, but the humble in spirit will retain honor.

Proverbs 29:23 (NKJV)

There are those – how lofty are their eyes, how high their eyelids lift!

Proverbs 30:13 (ESV)

If you have played the fool and exalted yourself, or if you have planned evil, clap your hand over your mouth!

Proverbs 30:32 (NIV)

Instruction

The proverbs of Solomon the son of David, king of Israel: to know wisdom and instruction, to perceive the words of understanding, to receive the instruction of wisdom, justice, judgment, and equity; to give prudence to the simple, to the young man knowledge and discretion – a wise man will hear and increase learning, and a man of understanding will attain wise counsel, to understand a proverb and an enigma, the words of the wise and their riddles. The fear of the Lord is the beginning of knowledge, but fools despise wisdom and instruction.

Proverbs 1:1-7 (NKJV)

My son, hear the instruction of thy father, and forsake not the law of thy mother.

Proverbs 1:8 (KJV)

My son, do not forget my law, but let your heart keep my commands.

Proverbs 3:1 (NKJV)

Instruction

Hear, O sons, a father's instruction, and be attentive, that you may gain insight, for I give you good precepts; do not forsake my teaching. When I was a son with my father, tender, the only one in the sight of my mother, he taught me and said to me, "Let your heart hold fast my words; keep my command-ments, and live. Get wisdom; get insight; do not forget, and do not turn away from the words of my mouth."

Proverbs 4:1-5 (ESV)

Take fast hold of instruction; let her not go: keep her; for she is thy life.

Proverbs 4:13 (KJV)

He shall die for lack of instruction, and in the greatness of his folly he shall go astray.

Proverbs 5:23 (NKJV)

Instruction

For the commandment is a lamp; and the law is light; and reproofs of instruction are the way of life.

Proverbs 6:23 (KJV)

Choose my instruction instead of silver, knowledge rather than choice gold, for wisdom is more precious than rubies, and nothing you desire can compare with her.

Proverbs 8:10-11 (NIV)

Give instruction to a wise man, and he will be still wiser; teach a just man, and he will increase in learning.

Proverbs 9:9 (NKJV)

Whoever heeds instruction is on the path to life, but he who rejects reproof leads others astray.

Proverbs 10:17 (ESV)

A wise son heareth his father's instruction: but a scorner heareth not rebuke.

Proverbs 13:1 (KJV)

Poverty and shame will come to him who disdains correction, but he who regards a rebuke will be honored.

Proverbs 13:18 (NKJV)

Whoever ignores instruction despises himself, but he who listens to reproof gains intelligence.

Proverbs 15:32 (ESV)

Cease listening to instruction, my son, and you will stray from the words of knowledge.

Proverbs 19:27 (NKJV)

When a mocker is punished, the simple gain wisdom; when a wise man is instructed, he gets knowledge.

Proverbs 21:11 (NIV)

Integrity

For the upright will dwell in the land, and the blameless will remain in it; but the wicked will be cut off from the earth, and the unfaithful will be uprooted from it.

Proverbs 2:21-22 (NKJV)

He who walks with integrity walks securely, but he who perverts his ways will become known.

Proverbs 10:9 (NKJV)

The integrity of the upright guides them, but the crookedness of the treacherous destroys them.

Proverbs 11:3 (ESV)

Righteousness guards the man of integrity, but wickedness overthrows the sinner.

Proverbs 13:6 (NIV)

The house of the wicked will be destroyed, but the tent of the upright will flourish.

Proverbs 14:11 (ESV)

The highway of the upright is to depart from evil; he who keeps his way preserves his soul.

Proverbs 16:17 (NKJV)

It is not good to punish an innocent man, or to flog officials for their integrity.

Proverbs 17:26 (NIV)

Better is a poor person who walks in his integrity than one who is crooked in speech and is a fool.

Proverbs 19:1 (ESV)

The just man walketh in his integrity: his children are blessed after him.

Proverbs 20:7 (KJV)

Even a child is known by his deeds, whether what he does is pure and right.

Proverbs 20:11 (NKJV)

Integrity

The way of the guilty is crooked, but the conduct of the pure is upright.

Proverbs 21:8 (ESV)

A wicked man hardeneth his face: but as for the upright, he directeth his way.

Proverbs 21:29 (KJV)

Better is a poor man who walks in his integrity than a rich man who is crooked in his ways.

Proverbs 28:6 (ESV)

Bloodthirsty men hate a man of integrity and seek to kill the upright.

Proverbs 29:10 (NIV)

An unjust man is an abomination to the righteous, and he who is upright in the way is an abomination to the wicked.

Proverbs 29:27 (NKJV)

Jealousy

Envy thou not the oppressor, and choose none of his ways. For the froward is abomination to the LORD: but his secret is with the righteous.

Proverbs 3:31-32 (KJV)

He who commits adultery lacks sense. Wounds and dishonor will he get, and his disgrace will not be wiped away. For jealousy makes a man furious, and he will not spare when he takes revenge.

Proverbs 6:32-34 (ESV)

A sound heart is the life of the flesh: but envy the rottenness of the bones.

Proverbs 14:30 (KJV)

Do not let your heart envy sinners, but always be zealous for the fear of the LORD. There is surely a future hope for you, and your hope will not be cut off.

Proverbs 23:17-18 (NIV)

Jealousy

Do not envy wicked men, do not desire their company; for their hearts plot violence, and their lips talk about making trouble.

Proverbs 24:1-2 (NIV)

Do not fret because of evildoers, nor be envious of the wicked; for there will be no prospect for the evil man; the lamp of the wicked will be put out.

Proverbs 24:19-20 (NKJV)

Wrath is cruel, and anger is outrageous; but who is able to stand before envy?

Proverbs 27:4 (KJV)

Death and Destruction are never satisfied, and neither are the eyes of man.

Proverbs 27:20 (NIV)

Let thy fountain be blessed: and rejoice with the wife of thy youth.

Proverbs 5:18 (KJV)

A wise son makes a glad father, but a foolish son is the grief of his mother.

Proverbs 10:1 (NKJV)

The prospect of the righteous is joy, but the hopes of the wicked come to nothing.

Proverbs 10:28 (NIV)

Deceit is in the heart of those who devise evil, but those who plan peace have joy.

Proverbs 12:20 (ESV)

Heaviness in the heart of man maketh it stoop: but a good word maketh it glad.

Proverbs 12:25 (KJV)

A cheerful look brings joy to the heart, and good news gives health to the bones.

Proverbs 15:30 (NIV)

Joy and gladness

It is a joy for the just to do justice, but destruction will come to the workers of iniquity.

Proverbs 21:15 (NKJV)

My son, if thine heart be wise, my heart shall rejoice, even mine. Yea, my reins shall rejoice, when thy lips speak right things.

Proverbs 23:15-16 (KJV)

The father of a righteous man has great joy; he who has a wise son delights in him. May your father and mother be glad; may she who gave you birth rejoice!

Proverbs 23:24-25 (NIV)

Do not rejoice when your enemy falls, and let not your heart be glad when he stumbles, lest the LORD see it and be displeased, and turn away his anger from him.

Proverbs 24:17-18 (ESV)

Ointment and perfume rejoice the heart: so doth the sweetness of a man's friend by hearty counsel.

Proverbs 27:9 (KJV)

Be wise, my son, and bring joy to my heart; then I can answer anyone who treats me with contempt.

Proverbs 27:11 (NIV)

When the righteous rejoice, there is great glory; but when the wicked arise, men hide themselves.

Proverbs 28:12 (NKJV)

When the righteous are in authority, the people rejoice: but when the wicked beareth rule, the people mourn.

Proverbs 29:2 (KJV)

Strength and honour are her clothing; and she shall rejoice in time to come.

Proverbs 31:25 (KJV)

Judgment

He keepeth the paths of judgment, and preserveth the way of his saints. Then shalt thou
understand righteousness, and judgment,
and equity; yea, every good path.

Proverbs 2:8-9 (KJV)

I walk in the way of righteousness, along the
paths of justice, bestowing wealth on those
who love me and making their treasuries
full.

Proverbs 8:20-21 (NIV)

Much food is in the tillage of the poor: but
there is that is destroyed for want of judgment.

Proverbs 13:23 (KJV)

The wicked accepts a bribe in secret to pervert
the ways of justice.

Proverbs 17:23 (ESV)

It is not good to punish an innocent man, or to flog officials for their integrity.

Proverbs 17:26 (NIV)

It is not good to accept the person of the wicked, to overthrow the righteous in judgment.

Proverbs 18:5 (KJV)

A worthless witness mocks at justice, and the mouth of the wicked devours iniquity.

Proverbs 19:28 (ESV)

To do justice and judgment is more acceptable to the LORD than sacrifice.

Proverbs 21:3 (KJV)

The violence of the wicked will destroy them, because they refuse to do justice.

Proverbs 21:7 (NKJV)

Judgment

When justice is done, it brings joy to the righteous but terror to evildoers.

Proverbs 21:15 (NIV)

These things also belong to the wise. It is not good to have respect of persons in judgment.

Proverbs 24:23 (KJV)

Those who forsake the law praise the wicked, but those who keep the law resist them. Evil men do not understand justice, but those who seek the LORD understand it fully.

Proverbs 28:4-5 (NIV)

Many seek the face of a ruler, but it is from the LORD that a man gets justice.

Proverbs 29:26 (ESV)

Open your mouth, judge righteously, defend the rights of the poor and needy.

Proverbs 31:9 (ESV)

The fear of the LORD is the beginning of knowledge; fools despise wisdom and instruction.

Proverbs 1:7 (ESV)

How long, ye simple ones, will ye love simplicity and the scorners delight in their scorning, and fools hate knowledge?

Proverbs 1:22 (KJV)

My son, if you accept my words and store up my commands within you, and if you call out for insight and cry aloud for understanding, then you will understand the fear of the LORD and find the knowledge of God.

Proverbs 2:1, 3, 5 (NIV)

The LORD by wisdom founded the earth; by understanding He established the heavens; by His knowledge the depths were broken up, and clouds drop down the dew.

Proverbs 3:19-20 (NKJV)

Knowledge

My son, pay attention to my wisdom, listen well to my words of insight, that you may maintain discretion and your lips may preserve knowledge.

Proverbs 5:1-2 (NIV)

All the words of my mouth are righteous; there is nothing twisted or crooked in them. They are all straight to him who understands, and right to those who find knowledge. I, wisdom, dwell with prudence, and I find knowledge and discretion.

Proverbs 8:8-9, 12 (ESV)

Wise men lay up knowledge: but the mouth of the foolish is near destruction.

Proverbs 10:14 (KJV)

The hypocrite with his mouth destroys his neighbor, but through knowledge the righteous will be delivered.

Proverbs 11:9 (NKJV)

A prudent man concealeth knowledge: but the heart of fools proclaimeth foolishness.

Proverbs 12:23 (KJV)

A scoffer seeks wisdom in vain, but knowledge is easy for a man of understanding.

Proverbs 14:6 (ESV)

He who has knowledge spares his words, and a man of understanding is of a calm spirit.

Proverbs 17:27 (NKJV)

An intelligent heart acquires knowledge, and the ear of the wise seeks knowledge.

Proverbs 18:15 (ESV)

It is not good to have zeal without knowledge, nor to be hasty and miss the way.

Proverbs 19:2 (NIV)

Knowledge

When a scoffer is punished, the simple becomes wise; when a wise man is instructed, he gains knowledge.

Proverbs 21:11 (ESV)

The eyes of the LORD preserve knowledge, and he overthroweth the words of the transgressor.

Proverbs 22:12 (KJV)

By wisdom a house is built, and through understanding it is established; through knowledge its rooms are filled with rare and beautiful treasures.

Proverbs 24:3-4 (NIV)

So shall the knowledge of wisdom be unto thy soul: when thou hast found it, then there shall be a reward, and thy expectation shall not be cut off.

Proverbs 24:14 (KJV)

Go to the ant, you sluggard; consider its ways and be wise! It has no commander, no overseer or ruler, yet it stores its provisions in summer and gathers its food at harvest. How long will you lie there, you sluggard? When will you get up from your sleep? A little sleep, a little slumber, a little folding of the hands to rest – and poverty will come on you like a bandit and scarcity like an armed man.

Proverbs 6:6-11 (NIV)

As vinegar to the teeth so is the sluggard to them that send him.

Proverbs 10:26 (KJV)

The hand of the diligent will rule, while the slothful will be put to forced labor.

Proverbs 12:24 (ESV)

Whoever is slothful will not roast his game, but the diligent man will get precious wealth.

Proverbs 12:27 (ESV)

Laziness

The soul of a lazy man desires, and has nothing; but the soul of the diligent shall be made rich.

Proverbs 13:4 (NKJV)

The way of the slothful man is as an hedge of thorns: but the way of the righteous is made plain.

Proverbs 15:19 (KJV)

Whoever is slack in his work is a brother to him who destroys.

Proverbs 18:9 (ESV)

Laziness brings on deep sleep, and the shiftless man goes hungry.

Proverbs 19:15 (NIV)

A lazy man buries his hand in the bowl, and will not so much as bring it to his mouth again.

Proverbs 19:24 (NKJV)

The sluggard will not plow by reason of the cold; therefore shall he beg in harvest, and have nothing.

Proverbs 20:4 (KJV)

The desire of the lazy man kills him, for his hands refuse to labor.

Proverbs 21:25 (NKJV)

As the door turneth upon his hinges, so doth the slothful upon his bed.

Proverbs 26:14 (KJV)

The lazy man is wiser in his own eyes than seven men who can answer sensibly.

Proverbs 26:16 (NKJV)

A little sleep, a little slumber, a little folding of the hands to rest – and poverty will come on you like a bandit and scarcity like an armed man.

Proverbs 24:33-34 (NIV)

Such are the ways of everyone who is greedy for unjust gain; it takes away the life of its possessors.

Proverbs 1:19 (ESV)

My son, do not forget my law, but let your heart keep my commands; for length of days and long life and peace they will add to you.

Proverbs 3:1-2 (NKJV)

For whoever finds me finds life, and obtains favor from the LORD.

Proverbs 8:35 (NKJV)

For by me thy days shall be multiplied, and the years of thy life shall be increased.

Proverbs 9:11 (KJV)

As righteousness leads to life, so he who pursues evil pursues it to his own death.

Proverbs 11:19 (NKJV)

In the path of righteousness is life, and in its pathway there is no death.

Proverbs 12:28 (ESV)

The fear of the LORD is a fountain of life, to depart from the snares of death.

Proverbs 14:27 (KJV)

The path of life leads upward for the wise to keep him from going down to the grave.

Proverbs 15:24 (NIV)

The fear of the LORD tendeth to life: and he that hath it shall abide satisfied.

Proverbs 19:23 (KJV)

He who follows righteousness and mercy finds life, righteousness and honor.

Proverbs 21:21 (NKJV)

The reward for humility and fear of the LORD is riches and honor and life.

Proverbs 22:4 (ESV)

Love

Let love and faithfulness never leave you; bind them around your neck, write them on the tablet of your heart. Then you will win favor and a good name in the sight of God and man.

Proverbs 3:3-4 (NIV)

My son, do not despise the chastening of the LORD, nor detest His correction; for whom the LORD loves He corrects, just as a father the son in whom he delights.

Proverbs 3:11-12 (NKJV)

I love those who love me, and those who seek me diligently find me.

Proverbs 8:17 (ESV)

I walk in the way of righteousness, along the paths of justice, bestowing wealth on those who love me and making their treasuries full.

Proverbs 8:20-21 (NIV)

Reprove not a scorner, lest he hate thee: rebuke a wise man, and he will love thee.

Proverbs 9:8 (KJV)

Hatred stirs up strife, but love covers all sins.

Proverbs 10:12 (NKJV)

Better is a dinner of herbs where love is, than a stalled ox and hatred therewith.

Proverbs 15:17 (KJV)

He who covers a transgression seeks love, but he who repeats a matter separates friends.

Proverbs 17:9 (NKJV)

A friend loveth at all times, and a brother is born for adversity.

Proverbs 17:17 (KJV)

Better is open rebuke than hidden love.

Proverbs 27:5 (NIV)

Lying

These six things the LORD hates, yes, seven are an abomination to Him: A proud look, a lying tongue, hands that shed innocent blood, a heart that devises wicked plans, feet that are swift in running to evil, a false witness who speaks lies, and one who sows discord among brethren.

Proverbs 6:16-19 (NKJV)

He that hideth hatred with lying lips, and he that uttereth a slander, is a fool.

Proverbs 10:18 (KJV)

The lip of truth shall be established for ever: but a lying tongue is but for a moment.

Proverbs 12:19 (KJV)

Lying lips are abomination to the LORD: but they that deal truly are his delight.

Proverbs 12:22 (KJV)

Lying

A righteous man hates lying, but a wicked man is loathsome and comes to shame.

Proverbs 13:5 (NKJV)

A faithful witness does not lie, but a false witness breathes out lies.

Proverbs 14:5 (ESV)

Excellent speech becometh not a fool: much less do lying lips a prince.

Proverbs 17:7 (KJV)

A false witness will not go unpunished, and he who speaks lies will not escape.

Proverbs 19:5 (NKJV)

A fortune made by a lying tongue is a fleeting vapor and a deadly snare.

Proverbs 21:6 (NIV)

A lying tongue hates its victims, and a flattering mouth works ruin.

Proverbs 26:28 (ESV)

Mercy

Let not mercy and truth forsake you; bind them around your neck, write them on the tablet of your heart, and so find favor and high esteem in the sight of God and man.

Proverbs 3:3-4 (NKJV)

The merciful man doeth good to his own soul: but he that is cruel troubleth his own flesh.

Proverbs 11:17 (KJV)

Whoever is righteous has regard for the life of his beast, but the mercy of the wicked is cruel.

Proverbs 12:10 (ESV)

Do they not err that devise evil? But mercy and truth shall be to them that devise good.

Proverbs 14:22 (KJV)

He who oppresses the poor reproaches his Maker, but he who honors Him has mercy on the needy.

Proverbs 14:31 (NKJV)

Mercy

In mercy and truth atonement is provided for iniquity; and by the fear of the LORD one departs from evil.

Proverbs 16:6 (NKJV)

He that hath pity upon the poor lendeth unto the LORD; and that which he hath given will he pay him again.

Proverbs 19:17 (KJV)

Mercy and truth preserve the king, and by lovingkindness he upholds his throne.

Proverbs 20:28 (NKJV)

He that by usury and unjust gain increaseth his substance, he shall gather it for him that will pity the poor.

Proverbs 28:8 (KJV)

He that covereth his sins shall not prosper: but whoso confesseth and forsaketh them shall have mercy.

Proverbs 28:13 (KJV)

Neighbors

Do not say to your neighbor, "Go, and come again, tomorrow I will give it" – when you have it with you.

Proverbs 3:28 (ESV)

Devise not evil against thy neighbour, seeing he dwelleth securely by thee.

Proverbs 3:29 (KJV)

He who despises his neighbor sins, but blessed is he who is kind to the needy.

Proverbs 14:21 (NIV)

A man lacking in judgment strikes hands in pledge and puts up security for his neighbor.

Proverbs 17:18 (NIV)

Be not a witness against thy neighbour without cause; and deceive not with thy lips.

Proverbs 24:28 (KJV)

Argue your case with your neighbor himself, and do not reveal another's secret, lest he who hears you bring shame upon you, and your ill repute have no end.

Proverbs 25:9-10 (ESV)

Like a club or a sword or a sharp arrow is the man who gives false testimony against his neighbor.

Proverbs 25:18 (NIV)

As a mad man who casteth firebrands, arrows, and death, so is the man that deceiveth his neighbour, and saith, Am not I in sport?

Proverbs 26:18-19 (KJV)

Thine own friend, and thy father's friend, forsake not; neither go into thy brother's house in the day of thy calamity: for better is a neighbour that is near than a brother far off.

Proverbs 27:10 (KJV)

Obedience

But whoever listens to me will dwell safely, and will be secure, without fear of evil.

Proverbs 1:33 (NKJV)

Hear, ye children, the instruction of a father, and attend to know understanding.

Proverbs 4:1 (KJV)

Hear, O my son, and receive my sayings; and the years of thy life shall be many.

Proverbs 4:10 (KJV)

My son, pay attention to my wisdom, listen well to my words of insight, that you may maintain discretion and your lips may preserve knowledge.

Proverbs 5:1-2 (NIV)

And now, O sons, listen to me, and do not depart from the words of my mouth.

Proverbs 5:7 (ESV)

Listen to my instruction and be wise; do not ignore it. Blessed is the man who listens to me, watching daily at my doors, waiting at my doorway.

Proverbs 8:33-34 (NIV)

The ear that heareth the reproof of life abideth among the wise.

Proverbs 15:31 (KJV)

Cease listening to instruction, my son, and you will stray from the words of knowledge.

Proverbs 19:27 (NKJV)

The hearing ear and the seeing eye, the LORD has made them both.

Proverbs 20:12 (ESV)

Bow down thine ear, and hear the words of the wise, and apply thine heart unto my knowledge.

Proverbs 22:17 (KJV)

Peace

Forget not my law; but let thine heart keep my commandments: For length of days, and long life, and peace, shall they add to thee.

Proverbs 3:1-2 (KJV)

Blessed is the man who finds wisdom, for she is more profitable than silver and yields better returns than gold. Her ways are pleasant ways, and all her paths are peace.

Proverbs 3:13-14, 17 (NIV)

He that is void of wisdom despiseth his neighbour: but a man of understanding holdeth his peace.

Proverbs 11:12 (KJV)

Deceit is in the heart of those who devise evil, but those who plan peace have joy.

Proverbs 12:20 (ESV)

A heart at peace gives life to the body, but envy rots the bones.

Proverbs 14:30 (NIV)

Peace

When a man's ways please the LORD, he makes even his enemies to be at peace with him.

Proverbs 16:7 (ESV)

Better a dry crust with peace and quiet than a house full of feasting, with strife.

Proverbs 17:1 (NIV)

Even a fool is counted wise when he holds his peace; when he shuts his lips, he is considered perceptive.

Proverbs 17:28 (NKJV)

If a wise man contendeth with a foolish man, whether he rage or laugh, there is no rest.

Proverbs 29:9 (KJV)

Discipline your son, and he will give you peace; he will bring delight to your soul.

Proverbs 29:17 (NIV)

Poverty and wealth

Honor the LORD with your possessions, and with the firstfruits of all your increase; so your barns will be filled with plenty, and your vats will overflow with new wine.

Proverbs 3:8-10 (NKJV)

Riches and honor are with me, enduring wealth and righteousness. My fruit is better than gold, even fine gold, and my yield than choice silver.

Proverbs 8:18-19 (ESV)

Lazy hands make a man poor, but diligent hands bring wealth.

Proverbs 10:4 (NIV)

A rich man's wealth is his strong city; the poverty of the poor is their ruin.

Proverbs 10:15 (ESV)

The blessing of the LORD makes one rich, and He adds no sorrow with it.

Proverbs 10:22 (NKJV)

There is that scattereth, and yet increaseth; and there is that withholdeth more than is meet, but it tendeth to poverty.

Proverbs 11:24 (KJV)

One man pretends to be rich, yet has nothing; another pretends to be poor, yet has great wealth.

Proverbs 13:7 (NIV)

Wealth gained by dishonesty will be diminished, but he who gathers by labor will increase.

Proverbs 13:11 (NKJV)

The poor is hated even of his own neighbour: but the rich hath many friends.

Proverbs 14:20 (KJV)

Better is little with the fear of the LORD than great treasure and trouble therewith.

Proverbs 15:16 (KJV)

Poverty and wealth

Wealth brings many new friends, but a poor man is deserted by his friend.

Proverbs 19:4 (ESV)

He who has pity on the poor lends to the LORD, and He will pay back what he has given.

Proverbs 19:17 (NKJV)

Love not sleep, lest thou come to poverty; open thine eyes, and thou shalt be satisfied with bread.

Proverbs 20:13 (KJV)

He who loves pleasure will be a poor man; he who loves wine and oil will not be rich.

Proverbs 21:16-17 (NKJV)

A good name is to be chosen rather than great riches, and favor is better than silver or gold.

Proverbs 22:1 (ESV)

Humility and the fear of the Lord bring wealth and honor and life.

Proverbs 22:4 (NIV)

He that oppresseth the poor to increase his riches, and he that giveth to the rich, shall surely come to want.

Proverbs 22:16 (KJV)

Whoever works his land will have plenty of bread, but he who follows worthless pursuits will have plenty of poverty.

Proverbs 28:19 (ESV)

A man with an evil eye hastens after riches, and does not consider that poverty will come upon him.

Proverbs 28:22 (NKJV)

Remove far from me vanity and lies: give me neither poverty nor riches; feed me with food convenient for me.

Proverbs 30:8 (KJV)

Reproof

If you turn at my reproof, behold, I will pour out my spirit to you; I will make my words known to you.

Proverbs 1:23 (ESV)

Since they hated knowledge and did not choose to fear the LORD, since they would not accept my advice and spurned my rebuke, they will eat the fruit of their ways and be filled with the fruit of their schemes.

Proverbs 1:29-31 (NIV)

My son, despise not the chastening of the LORD; neither be weary of his correction: For whom the LORD loveth he correcteth; even as a father the son in whom he delighteth.

Proverbs 3:11-12 (KJV)

Do not reprove a scoffer, or he will hate you; reprove a wise man, and he will love you.

Proverbs 9:8 (ESV)

He who keeps instruction is in the way of life, but he who refuses correction goes astray.

Proverbs 10:17 (NKJV)

Whoso loveth instruction loveth knowledge: but he that hateth reproof is brutish.

Proverbs 12:1 (KJV)

He who ignores discipline comes to poverty and shame, but whoever heeds correction is honored.

Proverbs 13:18 (NIV)

There is severe discipline for him who forsakes the way; whoever hates reproof will die.

Proverbs 15:10 (ESV)

The ear that heareth the reproof of life abideth among the wise. He that refuseth instruction despiseth his own soul: but he that heareth reproof getteth understanding.

Proverbs 15:31-32 (KJV)

Reproof

When a scoffer is punished, the simple becomes wise; when a wise man is instructed, he gains knowledge.

Proverbs 21:11 (ESV)

Do not withhold correction from a child, for if you beat him with a rod, he will not die.

Proverbs 23:13 (NKJV)

A word fitly spoken is like apples of gold in a setting of silver. Like a gold ring or an ornament of gold is a wise reprover to a listening ear.

Proverbs 25:11-12 (ESV)

The rod of correction imparts wisdom, but a child left to himself disgraces his mother.

Proverbs 29:15 (NIV)

Correct thy son, and he shall give thee rest; yea, he shall give delight unto thy soul.

Proverbs 29:17 (KJV)

So you will walk in the way of the good and keep to the paths of the righteous.

Proverbs 2:20 (ESV)

The curse of the LORD is in the house of the wicked: but he blesseth the habitation of the just.

Proverbs 3:33 (KJV)

The path of the righteous is like the first gleam of dawn, shining ever brighter till the full light of day. But the way of the wicked is like deep darkness; they do not know what makes them stumble.

Proverbs 4:18-19 (NIV)

Blessings are on the head of the righteous, but violence covers the mouth of the wicked. The memory of the righteous is blessed, but the name of the wicked will rot.

Proverbs 10:6-7 (NKJV)

Righteousness

What the wicked dreads will overtake him; what the righteous desire will be granted. When the storm has swept by, the wicked are gone, but the righteous stand firm forever.

Proverbs 10:24-25 (NIV)

Though they join forces, the wicked will not go unpunished; but the posterity of the righteous will be delivered.

Proverbs 11:21 (NKJV)

The fruit of the righteous is a tree of life; and he that winneth souls is wise. The righteous shall be recompensed in the earth.

Proverbs 11:30-31 (KJV)

The thoughts of the righteous are right, but the counsels of the wicked are deceitful. The words of the wicked are, "Lie in wait for blood," but the mouth of the upright will deliver them.

Proverbs 12:5-6 (NKJV)

In the way of righteousness is life; and in the pathway thereof there is no death.

Proverbs 12:28 (KJV)

A righteous man hates lying, but a wicked man is loathsome and comes to shame. Righteousness guards him whose way is blameless, but wickedness overthrows the sinner.

Proverbs 13:5-6 (NKJV)

Evil pursueth sinners: but to the righteous good shall be repaid.

Proverbs 13:21 (KJV)

The righteous has enough to satisfy his appetite, but the belly of the wicked suffers want.

Proverbs 13:25 (ESV)

The wicked is driven away in his wickedness: but the righteous hath hope in his death.

Proverbs 14:32 (KJV)

Righteousness

The house of the righteous contains great treasure, but the income of the wicked brings them trouble.

Proverbs 15:6 (NIV)

He that justifieth the wicked, and he that condemneth the just, even they both are abomination to the LORD.

Proverbs 17:15 (KJV)

The name of the LORD is a strong tower; the righteous man runs into it and is safe.

Proverbs 18:10 (ESV)

The righteous God wisely considers the house of the wicked, overthrowing the wicked for their wickedness.

Proverbs 21:12 (NKJV)

An evil man is ensnared in his transgression, but a righteous man sings and rejoices.

Proverbs 29:6 (ESV)

The wise shall inherit glory: but shame shall be the promotion of fools.

Proverbs 3:35 (KJV)

But a man who commits adultery lacks judgment; whoever does so destroys himself. Blows and disgrace are his lot, and his shame will never be wiped away.

Proverbs 6:32-33 (NIV)

He who corrects a scoffer gets shame for himself, and he who rebukes a wicked man only harms himself.

Proverbs 9:7 (NKJV)

He who gathers in summer is a prudent son, but he who sleeps in harvest is a son who brings shame.

Proverbs 10:5 (ESV)

Shame

A fool's wrath is presently known: but a prudent man covereth shame.

Proverbs 12:16 (KJV)

The righteous hates falsehood, but the wicked brings shame and disgrace.

Proverbs 13:5 (ESV)

A king delights in a wise servant, but a shameful servant incurs his wrath.

Proverbs 14:35 (NIV)

A servant who deals wisely will rule over a son who acts shamefully and will share the inheritance as one of the brothers.

Proverbs 17:2 (ESV)

When wickedness comes, so does contempt, and with shame comes disgrace.

Proverbs 18:3 (NIV)

Shame

He who answers a matter before he hears it, it is folly and shame to him.

Proverbs 18:13 (NKJV)

He who robs his father and drives out his mother is a son who brings shame and disgrace.

Proverbs 19:26 (NIV)

Do not go hastily to court; for what will you do in the end, when your neighbor has put you to shame? Debate your case with your neighbor, and do not disclose the secret to another; lest he who hears it expose your shame, and your reputation be ruined.

Proverbs 25:8-10 (NKJV)

The one who keeps the law is a son with understanding, but a companion of gluttons shames his father.

Proverbs 28:7 (ESV)

Do not be wise in your own eyes; fear the LORD and shun evil. This will bring health to your body and nourishment to your bones.

Proverbs 3:7-8 (NIV)

My son, be attentive to my words; incline your ear to my sayings. Let them not escape from your sight; keep them within your heart. For they are life to those who find them, and healing to all their flesh.

Proverbs 4:20-22 (ESV)

The merciful man doeth good to his own soul: but he that is cruel troubleth his own flesh.

Proverbs 11:17 (KJV)

An excellent wife is the crown of her husband, but she who causes shame is like rottenness in his bones.

Proverbs 12:4 (NKJV)

There is that speaketh like the piercings of a sword: but the tongue of the wise is health.

Proverbs 12:18 (KJV)

Hope deferred makes the heart sick, but a longing fulfilled is a tree of life.

Proverbs 13:12 (NIV)

A wicked messenger falls into trouble, but a faithful envoy brings healing.

Proverbs 13:17 (ESV)

A sound heart is life to the body, but envy is rottenness to the bones.

Proverbs 14:30 (NKJV)

A cheerful look brings joy to the heart, and good news gives health to the bones.

Proverbs 15:30 (NIV)

Gracious words are like a honeycomb, sweetness to the soul and health to the body.

Proverbs 16:24 (ESV)

Sickness

A merry heart does good, like medicine, but a broken spirit dries the bones.

Proverbs 17:22 (NKJV)

Do not look at wine when it is red, when it sparkles in the cup and goes down smoothly. In the end it bites like a serpent and stings like an adder. You will be like one who lies down in the midst of the sea, like one who lies on the top of a mast. "They struck me," you will say, "but I was not hurt; they beat me, but I did not feel it. When shall I awake? I must have another drink."

Proverbs 23:31-32, 34-35 (ESV)

My son, if sinners entice you, do not consent. My son, do not walk in the way with them; hold back your foot from their paths, for their feet run to evil, and they make haste to shed blood.

Proverbs 1:10, 15-16 (ESV)

The evil deeds of a wicked man ensnare him; the cords of his sin hold him fast. He will die for lack of discipline, led astray by his own great folly.

Proverbs 5:22-23 (NIV)

But he who sins against me wrongs his own soul; all those who hate me love death?

Proverbs 8:36 (NKJV)

The labour of the righteous tendeth to life: the fruit of the wicked to sin.

Proverbs 10:16 (KJV)

When words are many, transgression is not lacking.

Proverbs 10:19 (ESV)

An evil man is trapped by his sinful talk, but a righteous man escapes trouble.

Proverbs 12:13 (NIV)

Righteousness guards him whose way is blameless, but sin overthrows the wicked.

Proverbs 13:6 (ESV)

He who despises his neighbor sins; but he who has mercy on the poor, happy is he.

Proverbs 14:21 (NKJV)

Righteousness exalts a nation, but sin is a disgrace to any people.

Proverbs 14:34 (NIV)

Who can say, "I have made my heart pure; I am clean from my sin"?

Proverbs 20:9 (ESV)

Put away perversity from your mouth; keep corrupt talk far from your lips.

Proverbs 4:24 (NIV)

A worthless person, a wicked man, goes about with crooked speech.

Proverbs 6:12 (ESV)

Blessings are on the head of the righteous, but violence covers the mouth of the wicked.

Proverbs 10:6 (NKJV)

The mouth of the righteous is a well of life, but violence covers the mouth of the wicked.

Proverbs 10:11 (NKJV)

The tongue of the just is as choice silver: the heart of the wicked is little worth. The lips of the righteous feed many: but fools die for want of wisdom.

Proverbs 10:20-21 (KJV)

Speech

The mouth of the righteous brings forth wisdom, but the perverse tongue will be cut out. The lips of the righteous know what is acceptable, but the mouth of the wicked what is perverse.

Proverbs 10:31-32 (NKJV)

With his mouth the godless man would destroy his neighbor, but by knowledge the righteous are delivered.

Proverbs 11:9 (ESV)

From the fruit of his lips a man is filled with good things as surely as the work of his hands rewards him.

Proverbs 12:14 (NIV)

There is one whose rash words are like sword thrusts, but the tongue of the wise brings healing. Truthful lips endure forever, but a lying tongue is but for a moment.

Proverbs 12:18-19 (ESV)

The tongue of the wise useth knowledge aright: but the mouth of fools poureth out foolishness. A wholesome tongue is a tree of life: but perverseness therein is a breach in the spirit.

Proverbs 15:2, 4 (KJV)

To make an apt answer is a joy to a man, and a word in season, how good it is!

Proverbs 15:23 (ESV)

The thoughts of the wicked are an abomination to the LORD, but the words of the pure are pleasant.

Proverbs 15:26 (NKJV)

A wise man's heart guides his mouth, and his lips promote instruction. Pleasant words are a honeycomb, sweet to the soul and healing to the bones.

Proverbs 16:23-24 (NIV)

Speech

An ungodly man diggeth up evil: and in his lips there is as a burning fire.

Proverbs 16:27 (KJV)

Death and life are in the power of the tongue, and those who love it will eat its fruits.

Proverbs 18:21 (ESV)

A fortune made by a lying tongue is a fleeting vapor and a deadly snare.

Proverbs 21:6 (NIV)

Like a madman who throws firebrands, arrows, and death, is the man who deceives his neighbor, and says, "I was only joking!"

Proverbs 26:18-19 (NKJV)

He that hateth dissembleth with his lips, and layeth up deceit within him; when he speaketh fair, believe him not: for there are seven abominations in his heart.

Proverbs 26:24-25 (KJV)

Then you will understand righteousness and justice and equity, every good path; for wisdom will come into your heart, and knowledge will be pleasant to your soul.

Proverbs 2:9-10 (ESV)

Blessed is the man who finds wisdom, the man who gains understanding.

Proverbs 3:13 (NIV)

My son, let not them depart from thine eyes: keep sound wisdom and discretion.

Proverbs 3:21 (KJV)

Get wisdom; get insight; do not forget, and do not turn away from the words of my mouth.

Proverbs 4:5 (ESV)

Wisdom is the principal thing; therefore get wisdom. And in all your getting, get understanding.

Proverbs 4:7 (NKJV)

Wisdom

I guide you in the way of wisdom and lead you along straight paths.

Proverbs 4:11 (NIV)

For wisdom is better than rubies; and all the things that may be desired are not to be compared to it. I wisdom dwell with prudence, and find out knowledge of witty inventions.

Proverbs 8:11-12 (KJV)

Counsel is mine, and sound wisdom: I am understanding; I have strength.

Proverbs 8:14 (KJV)

The fear of the LORD is the beginning of wisdom, and the knowledge of the Holy One is insight.

Proverbs 9:10 (ESV)

Wisdom is found on the lips of him who has understanding, but a rod is for the back of him who is devoid of understanding.

Proverbs 10:13 (NKJV)

A fool finds pleasure in evil conduct, but a man of understanding delights in wisdom.

Proverbs 10:23 (NIV)

A scoffer seeks wisdom in vain, but knowledge is easy for a man of understanding.

Proverbs 14:6 (ESV)

The fear of the LORD is the instruction of wisdom; and before honour is humility.

Proverbs 15:33 (KJV)

How much better to get wisdom than gold! And to get understanding is to be chosen rather than silver.

Proverbs 16:16 (NKJV)

A wise servant will rule over a disgraceful son, and will share the inheritance as one of the brothers.

Proverbs 17:2 (NIV)

Wisdom

A man's wisdom gives him patience; it is to his glory to overlook an offense.

Proverbs 19:11 (NIV)

No wisdom, no understanding, no counsel can avail against the LORD.

Proverbs 21:30 (ESV)

Bow down thine ear, and hear the words of the wise, and apply thine heart unto my knowledge.

Proverbs 22:17 (KJV)

Through wisdom a house is built, and by understanding it is established; by knowledge the rooms are filled with all precious and pleasant riches.

Proverbs 24:3-4 (NKJV)

He that trusteth in his own heart is a fool: but whoso walketh wisely, he shall be delivered.

Proverbs 28:26 (KJV)